To all the fangirls of the world,
keep fangirling—TC
To all Beyhive around the world—CM

PENGUIN WORKSHOP
An imprint of Penguin Random House LLC
1745 Broadway, New York, New York 10019

First published in the United States of America by Penguin Workshop,
an imprint of Penguin Random House LLC, 2025

Visit us online at penguinrandomhouse.com.

Library of Congress Cataloging-in-Publication Data is available.

Manufactured in China

ISBN 9798217052080
10 9 8 7 6 5 4 3 2 1
HH

The text is set in Adobe Garamond Pro.
The art was created using a Wacom pen tablet and Adobe Photoshop.

Design by Taylor Abatiell

The authorized representative in the EU for product safety and compliance is Penguin Random House Ireland,
Morrison Chambers, 32 Nassau Street, Dublin D02 YH68, Ireland, https://eu-contact.penguin.ie.

BEYONCÉ

A Who Was? ILLUSTRATED BIOGRAPHY

by
Tyiana Combs

illustrated by
Claudia Marianno

PENGUIN WORKSHOP

On a warm May evening in 2023, nearly one hundred thousand fans packed Friends Arena in Stockholm, Sweden. Decked out in shimmering silver, sequins, and sparkles, they had anticipated for months and traveled miles to witness the performer's first tour in five years.

Crafted with detail, patience, and a nod to Afrofuturism, this tour would go on to become one of the most successful of all time.

Who was this performer about to make history?

Four decades earlier, on September 4, 1981, Beyoncé Giselle Knowles was born in Houston, Texas, to parents Mathew and Tina Knowles. Beyoncé's name was an ode to her mother's maiden name, and receiving it began a theme of honoring family legacy, something Beyoncé has continued to do throughout her life.

While she now exudes confidence, she was once a shy girl. According to her mother, she found it hard to come out of her shell and make friends, but she shone in dance class. One day, her dance teacher heard her singing and was in awe of her voice. From that moment, the trajectory of Beyoncé's life was forever changed.

Singing quickly became a staple in Beyoncé's life. "My voice has always been my companion," she said. She sang in choir at her school and church and as she worked her first job sweeping up hair in her mother's salon. Soon singing led her to audition for and join Girl's Tyme, a new group being formed in Houston. Girl's Tyme was so talented that they were placed in *Star Search*, a national televised talent show. Though they did not win, they did gain more exposure and a record deal.

Beyoncé's father would become the group's manager, quitting his job to focus on their budding career. While in the group, Beyoncé discovered how much she enjoyed writing songs as well as singing them. Despite the progress the group was making, they were dropped from their record label. But this was only the beginning.

In 1996, Girl's Tyme became Destiny's Child, hitting the scene with a new name, a new record deal, and, in 1997, a hit song: "No, No, No." Their first album, *Destiny's Child*, was released in 1998, and its follow-up, *The Writing's on the Wall*, would sell over eight million copies. It would also win the group their first Grammy Award, for the single "Say My Name."

By 2000, Destiny's Child would restructure into a trio consisting of Beyoncé, Kelly Rowland, and Michelle Williams. From there, the young women would go on to record and release the 2001 album *Survivor*, which was nominated for Best R&B Album at the Grammys and sold over three million copies by the end of the year.

As a group, Destiny's Child loved performing together, but they also wanted to take time to focus on solo projects. Beyoncé's first solo project was *Dangerously in Love*, released in 2003. Despite being doubted by both her label and critics, she was met with much success, including five hit singles and five Grammy wins in 2004. **Her debut album became one of the bestselling albums of the twenty-first century.**

The lyrics she wrote were heavily inspired by love, and the lead single would contain a feature from rapper Jay-Z. First collaborating on the 2002 single "'03 Bonnie & Clyde," Beyoncé and Jay-Z quickly became music peers and would often work together. Though many wondered if their relationship was both professional and personal, the pair kept it private.

Destiny's Child would reunite to record and release *Destiny Fulfilled* in 2004, but soon after made the mutual decision to part ways and continue their solo journeys. Beyoncé also began to act, and in 2006, she played Deena in *Dreamgirls*. The film was about an R&B girl group in the 1960s and 1970s, and it became a box office hit nominated for eight Oscars.

Filming *Dreamgirls* energized Beyoncé so much that she was inspired to create her second solo album, *B'Day*. For many artists, preparing their second album is stressful, and they can spend years trying to perfect it. But Beyoncé was able to craft a funk-inspired, genre-bending album in just a few weeks, and it won Best Contemporary R&B Album at the 2007 Grammys. It was a hit with reviewers, critics, and her growing fan base, the Beyhive.

Her winning streak continued the following year with the release of her third studio album, *I Am . . . Sasha Fierce*, a double album with elements of both Beyoncé and her alter ego, Sasha Fierce, the persona she would take on to feel more confident onstage. This album included one of her most well-known songs, "Single Ladies (Put a Ring on It)," and she soon earned the name "Queen Bey" for her dominance in the music industry.

Around this time, Beyoncé married Jay-Z and took a break from music to learn more about herself. Upon her return, audiences were treated to the album 4, her first album after becoming her own manager. The number four has always been special to Beyoncé; her birthday, her husband's birthday, their anniversary date, and her mother's birthday are on the fourth day of the month.

FEMINIST

Her fifth solo album, self-titled *Beyoncé*, came as a surprise. Following the birth of daughter Blue Ivy Carter in 2012 and inspired in part by new motherhood, *Beyoncé* released in December 2013 with no promotion, but included a music video for each song on the album. The lack of promotion did not delay fan excitement and within the first three days of its appearance, *Beyoncé* sold over six hundred thousand digital copies.

The album also solidified Beyoncé as a feminist icon. While support for women's equality had been present in her career from early singles like "Survivor" and "Independent Women, Part 1," her bold statement at the 2014 Video Music Awards encouraged a new generation of young girls and women to unapologetically embrace feminism

Standing up for what's right was nothing new to Beyoncé. In 2013, she established the BeyGOOD foundation, which has offered resources to natural disaster survivors and the unhoused, gifted scholarships to students, granted assistance to small businesses, and more. Beyoncé has also been an advocate for voting rights and a GLAAD honoree for her work as an LGBTQIA+ ally.

Three years after the establishment of
BeyGOOD and her self-titled album, Beyoncé
released her sixth studio album, *Lemonade*, and its
accompanying film. It remains one of Beyoncé's
most personal works—telling a story of love lost and
found, and honoring Black Southern culture in its
imagery—and is considered by some to be one of
the greatest albums of all time.

ON THE STAGE AND AROUND THE WORLD

Across the span of her decades-long career, Beyoncé has embarked on numerous world tours crossing countries and continents, performing hundreds of shows, including:

- Dangerously in Love Tour (2003, 10 shows)
- The Beyoncé Experience (2007, 96 shows)
- I Am . . . Tour (2009–2010, 108 shows)
- The Mrs. Carter Show World Tour (2013–2014, 132 shows)
- On the Run Tour (2014, 21 shows)
- The Formation World Tour (2016, 49 shows)
- On the Run II Tour (2018, 48 shows)
- Renaissance World Tour (2023, 56 shows)

Following the birth of twins Sir and Rumi in 2017, Beyoncé hit the stage again in April 2018, making history by becoming the first Black woman to be the main act at the music festival Coachella with a performance dubbed "Beychella," bringing the culture of Historically Black Colleges and Universities (HBCUs) to the stage. Beyoncé did not attend a traditional college. She said, "My college was Destiny's Child. My college was traveling around the world." Still, she had "always dreamed of going to an HBCU." Her performance, which also included guest appearances from her sister, Solange, and Destiny's Child, brought that dream to life and inspired her 2019 film "Homecoming."

After voicing Nala in the CGI version of *The Lion King* in 2019, Beyoncé curated and produced an album called *The Lion King: The Gift* to accompany the Disney movie and created her own film, *Black Is King*, as a visual for the album. She described the 2020 film, a retelling of *The Lion King* that explores and honors the African diaspora, as her passion project.

   Around the same time, Beyoncé would begin
work on her seventh studio album, *Renaissance*,
a dance album meant to get people moving,
celebrating, and enjoying life after the stress and
trauma of the COVID-19 pandemic. The album
also served as an ode to Black dance music and
Black queerness, dedicated to Beyoncé's Uncle
Johnny.

Renaissance became one of the best-rated albums of 2022 and served as the backdrop for the 2023 Renaissance World Tour, which had over two million fans in attendance across five months, each show nearly three hours long. Beyoncé's oldest daughter, Blue Ivy, joined her to dance onstage for multiple stops, imagery many working moms were inspired by. But *Renaissance* was only the first act of what Beyoncé had planned for the future.

Back in 2016, Beyoncé performed her song "Daddy Lessons" alongside country band the Chicks at the Country Music Awards. Despite the song being a country song, some country fans were not happy and declared that Beyoncé did not belong in their space. Rather than letting those criticisms stop her, Beyoncé took the next few years to craft a country-inspired album as the second act, *Cowboy Carter*, released in 2024.

Supported by singles "Texas Hold 'Em," which trended as a popular sound and dance for months on TikTok, and "16 Carriages," *Cowboy Carter* urged listeners to recognize the relationship between Blackness, Americana culture, and country music. Bringing together Black country musicians from the past and present, the album reminded audiences to keep an open mind when it comes to music. *Cowboy Carter* went to number one on the *Billboard* Top Country Albums chart, a first for a Black woman artist.

Beyoncé is a musician, a mother, a mogul, and a muse. Going from a young girl born in Houston, Texas, to being named the world's greatest living entertainer and one of the greatest vocalists of all time by *Rolling Stone*, Beyoncé is a true example of hard work, determination, drive, and betting on yourself.

BEYONCÉ BY THE NUMBERS

Over the course of her career, Beyoncé has received numerous awards and honors. Here are a few:

- Hundreds of award wins, including:
  - Thirty-two Grammy Awards, including six in 2010, the most wins in one night by a female artist at the time
  - One Peabody Award, for *Lemonade* in the Entertainment category, an award given to powerful stories in television, radio, and online media
- Over 1,300 award nominations, including eight Emmy nominations
- Eight *Billboard* 200 number one albums (*Billboard* 200 is a competitive chart ranking the two hundred most popular albums in the United States each week)

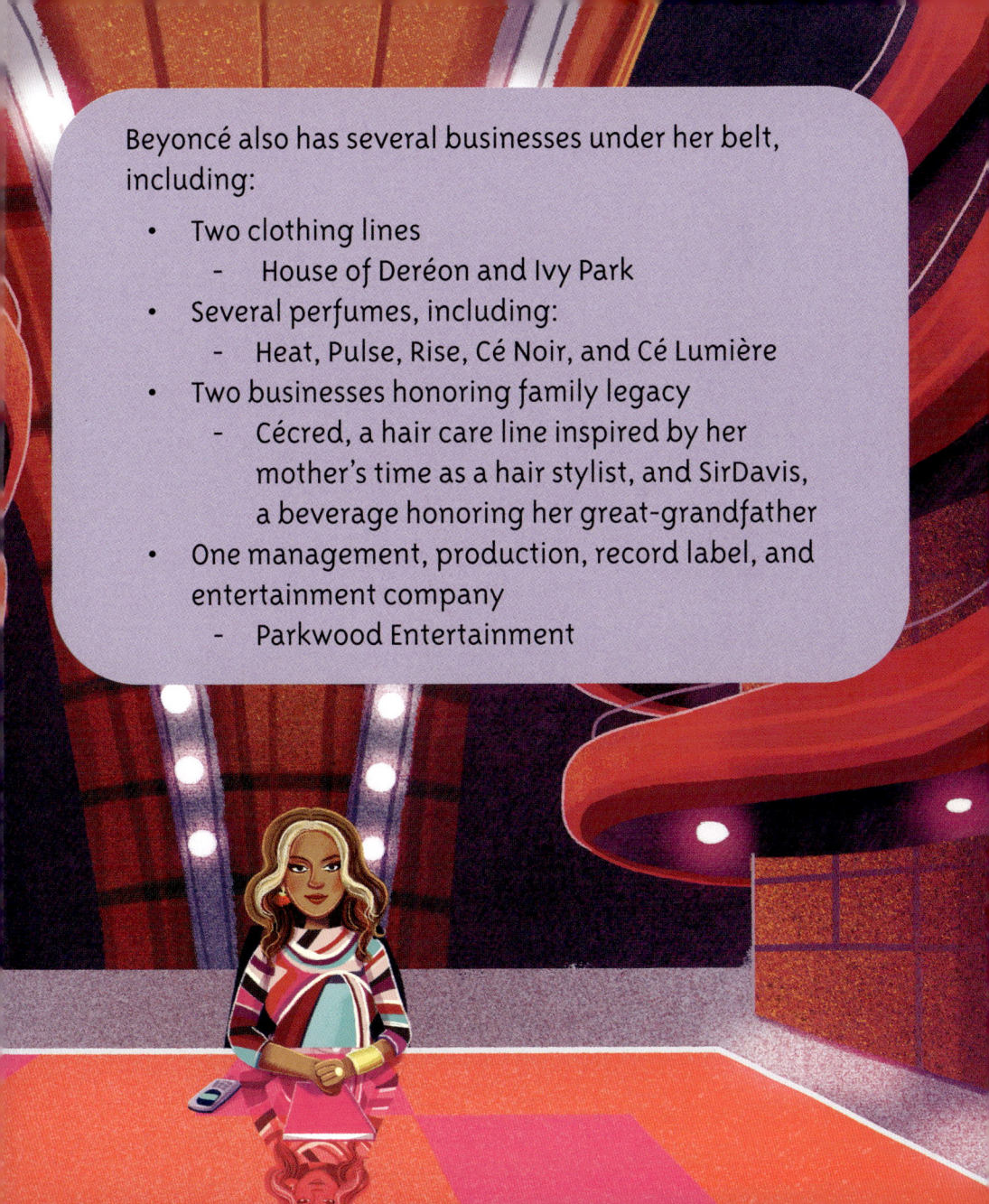

Beyoncé also has several businesses under her belt, including:

- Two clothing lines
    - House of Deréon and Ivy Park
- Several perfumes, including:
    - Heat, Pulse, Rise, Cé Noir, and Cé Lumière
- Two businesses honoring family legacy
    - Cécred, a hair care line inspired by her mother's time as a hair stylist, and SirDavis, a beverage honoring her great-grandfather
- One management, production, record label, and entertainment company
    - Parkwood Entertainment

Beyoncé has broken records, broken barriers, challenged audiences, and opened doors for the next generation of singers while honoring those who came before her, always making sure to give people their flowers. "I hope my work encourages people to look within themselves and come to terms with their own creativity, strength, and resilience." **With a career spanning four decades and counting, Beyoncé Giselle Knowles-Carter shows us that if we trust ourselves and our abilities, we can do anything.**

BIBLIOGRAPHY

*Books for young readers

Beyoncé, and Ed Burke, directors. *Homecoming: A Film by Beyoncé*. Netflix, 2019. https://www.netflix.com/title/81013626.

Chambers, Veronica. *Queen Bey: A Celebration of the Power and Creativity of Beyoncé Knowles-Carter*. New York: Picador, 2020.

*Lavette, Lavaille, and Anastasia Magloire Williams. *Beyoncé: A Little Golden Book Biography*. New York: Golden Books, 2023.

Tharpe, Frazier. "The Business of Being Beyoncé Knowles-Carter." *GQ*. September 10, 2024. https://www.gq.com/story/beyonce-knowles-carter-october-2024-cover-interview.

Tinsley, Omise'eke Natasha. *Beyoncé in Formation: Remixing Black Feminism*. Austin, TX: University of Texas Press, 2018.

WEBSITE

www.beyonce.com

TIMELINE

1981 — Beyoncé is born in Houston, Texas, on September 4

2001 — Destiny's Child wins their first Grammys for Best R&B song and Best R&B Performance by a Duo or Group with Vocal for "Say My Name"

2003 — Releases her first solo album, *Dangerously in Love*

2008 — Marries longtime partner Jay-Z; the pair will go on to have three children: Blue Ivy in 2012 and twins Rumi and Sir in 2017

Wins the Michael Jackson Video Vanguard Award, for "Outstanding Contributions" and "Profound Impact" on music videos and pop culture — **2014**

Wins the CFDA Fashion Icon Award — **2016**

Makes history by becoming the artist with the most Grammy Awards ever — **2023**

Named the greatest pop star of the twenty-first century by *Billboard* magazine — **2024**

Cowboy Carter wins Album of the Year and Best Country Album at the 67th Grammy Awards — **2025**